PEP THE POET

Poet & Well-being Champion

hello@pepthepoet.co.uk

Hello! I am David Ander Poet.
My mission is to 'scatter sunsh poem at a time.' I have written five poetry books for children. I deliver mental health, well-being and poetry workshops for schools, universities and corporates.

MY WORKSHOPS

POETRY WORKSHOPS

Ignite your creativity, build your confidence and find your inner voice through the power of poetry: Reciting, writing and performing.

WELL-BEING WORKSHOPS

From breakdown to breakthrough: Join me for an honest conversation on mental strength, finding yourself and facing the fears that hold us captive.

MY BOOKS

PETER PANTS

QUENTIN SQUIRREL

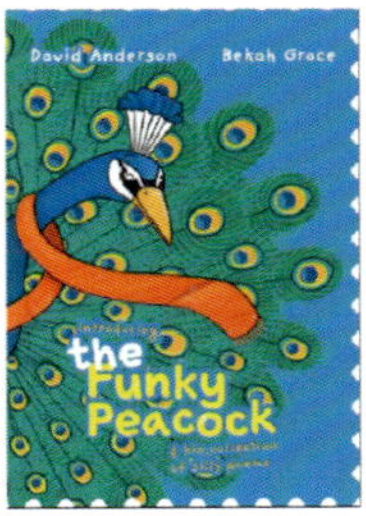

FUNKY PEACOCK

TINA ROBIN

LAUGHS & GIGGLES

"Pep is funny and brings poetry to life. He uses humour brilliantly to engage even the 'toughest' of reluctant poets."

~ J Kershaw, Y5 Teacher, Cannock

"Pep's work has a fundamental goodness about it, yet does not shy away from a little naughtiness."

~ T Rees Boughton, Retired Headteacher

The Dept. of
Laughs and Giggles

Just be brilliant
love

All poems written and illustrated by

David Anderson (aka Pep the Poet)

First published in 2023 by Dotty Edge
88 Eaton Drive, Rugeley, Staffordshire,
England, UK, WS15 2FS

This edition published in 2023

Typeset in Brandon Grotesque
Printed in the United Kingdom
ISBN Number 978-1-7396494-1-8
A catalogue record for this book is available from the British Library

Designed and formatted by Dotty Edge in the UK

www.pepthepoet.co.uk

The Dept. of
Laughs and Giggles

Contents

Page	
1	A to Z of School
2	Balla Balla Bourbon LeBeau
3	Beast of The Cubbyhole
4	Boofield Wellington Buzzel
5	Clark the Bark
6	Crocodilla-hollapog
7	Dear Mr Thompson
8	Department of Laughs and Giggles
10	Doctor, Doctor
12	Don't Wear a Kilt on Stilts
13	Ee By Gum
14	Goldilocks Has Lost the Plot
16	Granny's Time Machine
18	Guess What I Saw Today
19	Handy Aunty Hannah
19	Happy Families
20	Homework Homesick Blues
22	Horace the Hip Hop Horse
24	I've Got an Itch
25	I'm Grateful
26	I'm in Heaven With FD 1.1.11
28	I'm the Head and I'm in Charge!
32	If I Were
33	I Just Want to be a Plumber
34	I Love Ruby Russell
34	Imogen Crumbs
35	I Should Have Been a Superhero
36	It's 'Orrible Looking For Love When You're a Shark
38	Jane Frost
40	Jigsaw Pieces
41	Katie P – Our Brand New Striker
42	Limericks

Page	
43	Looking in the Mirror
44	Luck of the Drawer
48	Many
49	Monday Is Not a Fun Day
50	Noah's Long List
54	On it Like a Bard's Sonnet
56	On Me Holibobs!
58	Otto Signs for United
60	Pirate Problems
62	Pizza Toppings
63	Poetry Aerobics
64	Potatoes
65	Rebecca Decker
66	Sandra the Salamander
67	Scarlett's Magic Carpet
68	Thank You
70	The Factory Where Teachers Are Made
72	The Seagull Who Nicked My Chips
74	The Society of Funny Names
75	Told You I Was Ill
76	Two Hits to Who?
77	Uncle Fish
78	Vampire for Hire
80	Vicious Cycle
81	Walking in the Woods
82	What is Green?
83	What is Pink?
84	What's the Difference
85	Who Would Be a Referee?
86	Why do Dogs Sniff Bums?
87	Writer's Block
88	Yvonne My Pet Stone

A to Z of School

A is for attitude which you said we have loads.
B is for brains; you make ours explode.
C is for class and we're a class act.
D is for divide, times, add and subtract.
E is for the energy that our learning creates.
F is for the fastest one out of the gate.
G is the gym where we do our gymnastics.
H is for our homework, which isn't fantastic.
I is for independent which you'd like us to be.
J is for class joker, by the way, that's me.
K is for knowledge that you often impart.
L is for Lenny who does love to sing.
M is for maths for which I'm not able.
N is for naughty algebra and the 'B' times-table.
O is for office at the front of the school.
P is for parenthesis, a word that's just cruel.
Q is for queue, which we stand in at dinner.
R is for reflection that I see in the mirror.
S is for Science, RE, PE and Maths.
T is for its tables, pie charts and graphs.
U is for unhappy as I sit there at nine.
V is for very excited when I know it's home time.
W is for website, ours is quite cool.
X is for extracurricular - that stuff after school.
Y is for you Miss, as you're never wrong.
Z is for zoo where you said we belong.

So, this is our school from A to Z.
Please, don't believe all that I've said.
It's loved and adored by me and my friends.
Why not pop along and see for yourself.

Balla Balla Bourbon LeBeau

From the desert sands to the snows of Antarctica.
She's the real McCoy - the genuine article.
She turns their heads wherever she goes.
She's Balla Balla Bourbon LeBeau.

Her life is blessed and full of pleasure.
The wife of an Emperor with a terrible temper.
The Ice Goddess and Queen of the Snow.
She's Balla Balla Bourbon LeBeau.

A sleek black shawl over a snow-white gown.
Regal and respected but without the crown.
From whence she came, no one knows.
She's Balla Balla Bourbon LeBeau.

A skater. A dancer. A star of the sea.
Belly sliding, she does it with ease.
Wherever she goes, she's the star of the show.
She's Balla Balla Bourbon LeBeau.

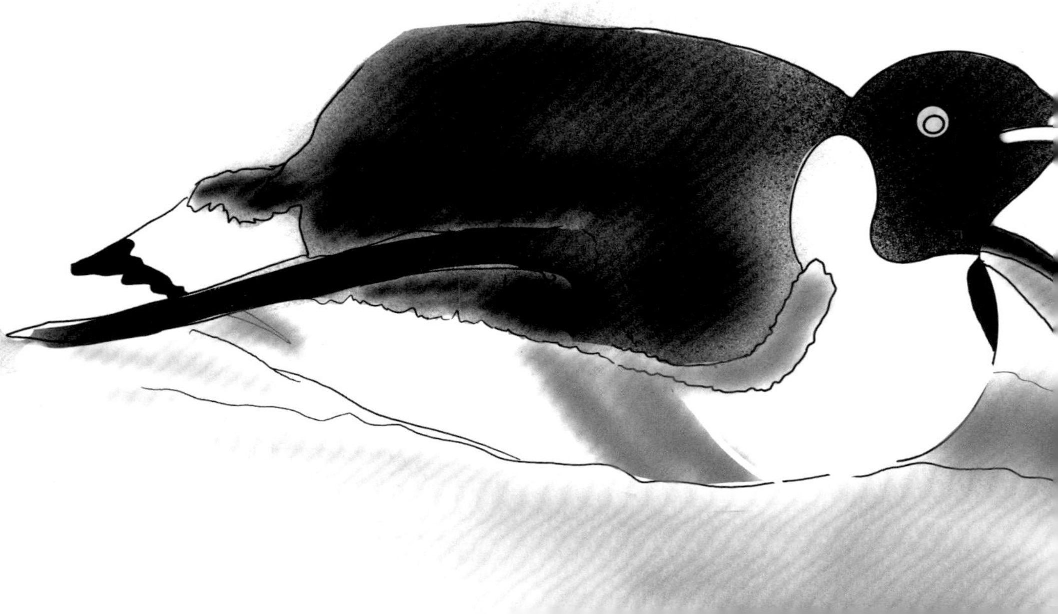

Beast of the Cubbyhole

I can't sleep or eat.
I'm getting thinner and thinner.
The Beast of the Cubbyhole.
Wants me for dinner!

I'm so frightened.
Since I heard the news.
My big brother says.
that it eats Year Twos.

There's a place in our house.
Where I never venture.
It's full of gruesome things.
I'm too frightened to mention.

Ghosts and spooks.
Yetis and ghouls.
A slimy green thing.
that spits and drools.

It's dark and it's dismal.
It serves no purpose at all.
The portal to Hell.
Right there in our hall.

It's full of old toys.
And broken dreams.
Smelly old trainers.
And something that screams.

"Don't you dare come in.
You have been told!
I'll gobble you up."
Roars the Beast of the Cubbyhole.

Boofield Wellington Buzzel

Boofield Wellington Buzzel
was very fond of puzzles,
he loved to sketch and draw.

With his pencils and crayons
he filled picture frames,
his sketches were all top drawer.

He drew the first thing
that entered his mind,
whether a frog, a dog or a mouse.

He loved his food
and when in the mood
he'd like to paint in the ... house.

Clark the Bark

Clark's the name, barking's the game.
I'll never give it up.
Itching and scratching, barking and farting.
I've done it since I was a pup.

Postal workers. Delivery drivers.
They're all petrified of me!
They cry and they moan when I chase them all home.
Then I have a bone for my tea.

I wasn't feeling too great when a feline called Grace.
Came strutting through my gate.
Stand aside Clark with your pathetic bark.
Was all I could hear her say.

I should let you all know that Grace runs the show.
She can floor me with a cutting remark.
She says I'm nothing too special, I should stay in my kennel.
I'm no longer Clark the Bark.

Crocodilla-Hollapog

He's big and strong and he's not too mean.
The friendliest monster that you've ever seen.
He's a little bit whacky and a little bit odd.
The Crocodilla, Crocodilla, Crocodilla-Hollapog.

He changes colour throughout the day.
From pastel pink to cold, slate-grey.
He likes his food really, really hot.
The Crocodilla, Crocodilla, Crocodilla-Hollapog.

He sleeps in a nest, in a cave underground.
He snores real quiet but trumps dead loud.
He wags his bottom like an excited dog.
The Crocodilla, Crocodilla, Crocodilla-Hollapog.

Don't be scared of my mate Crocky.
Deep, deep down he's just a big softie.
When he's nervous his words get muddled.
All he needs is a great big cuddle.

He doesn't brush his teeth and his breath is horrid.
His lips are green and his tongue bright orange.
He can jump real far, like an Olympic frog.
The Crocodilla, Crocodilla, Crocodilla-Hollapog.

He has scales on his back and fur on his belly.
Seven fingered hands and his feet are smelly.
He gets really drunk when he drinks Eggnog
The Crocodilla, Crocodilla, Crocodilla-Hollapog.

Claws on his feet and multi-coloured fingers
You know he's near as the smell it lingers.
He likes to fly to Spain for his holibobs.
The Crocodilla, Crocodilla, Crocodilla-Hollapog.

Dear Mr Thompson

Dear Mr Thompson,

Liam won't be in school today.
The reason why is hard to say.
He got up late and fell down the stairs
Trapped his nose in an old deckchair.
The dog bit him once or twice.
He slipped and fell upon the ice.
He trapped his hand in the bathroom door.
Caught the other in the kitchen drawer.
He burnt his mouth on a cup of tea.
Stubbed his toe when he went for a wee.
Dropped his homework in the kitchen bin.
Cut his finger on a rusty tin.
Stood in a puddle and wet his socks.
Caught mumps, measles and chickenpox.
Was bitten by a horse at next door's farm.
Fell off his bike and broke his arm.
I hope you understand my dear Mr Thompson
that coming to school just isn't an option.
I know my letter seems rather bleak.
I promise that Liam will be back next week.

Kind regards

Mr D Anderson
(Liam's Dad)

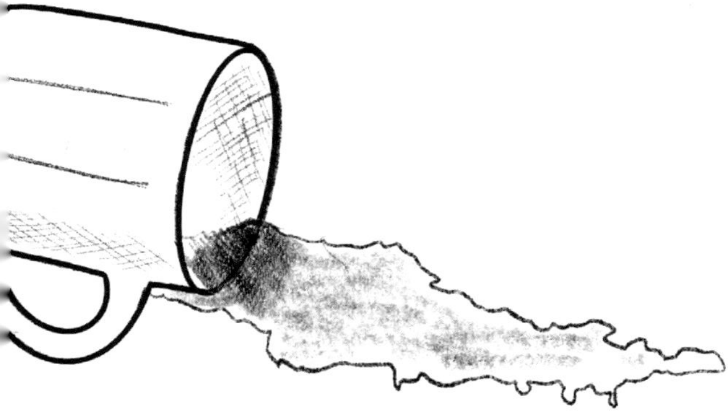

Department of Laughs and Giggles

Right smack bang in the middle of town.
There's a building where everyone goes.
It's full to the rafters with giggles and laughter.
You'll buzz in there from your head to your toes.
If your funny bones need a good tickle.
Then go to the Department of Giggles.

Knock Knock.
Who's there?
Lettuce,
Lettuce who?
Let us go to the Department of Giggles

It's totally whacky and really cool.
It's brilliance with bells and whistles.
In the Department of Laughs ...
In the Department of Laughs ...
In the Department of Laughs and Giggles.

The town's mayoress has always said,
It's illegal to be grumpy or sad.
You'll find her there, down in The Square,
Dancing like she's totally mad.
If you want to see her twist and swivel.
Then head to the Department of giggles.

Knock Knock.
Who's there?
Ima.
Ima who?
I'm a going to the Department of Giggles

It's totally whacky and really cool.
It's brilliance with bells and whistles.
In the Department of Laughs ...
In the Department of Laughs ...
In the Department of Laughs and Giggles.

The building is colossal, over seventeen floors.
It's funnier the higher you climb.
Beware on the sixth as you step from the lift
As you'll get covered with buckets of slime.
You can get free sweets right in the middle
Down in the Department of Giggles.

Knock. Knock.
Who's there?
Anita
Anita who?
I need to go to the Department of Giggles

It's totally whacky and really cool.
It's brilliance with bells and whistles.
In the Department of Laughs ...
In the Department of Laughs ...
In the Department of Laughs and Giggles.

Doctor, Doctor

Mrs Simpson:	Doctor, Doctor.
Doctor:	*(Bored)* Yes Mrs Simpson.
Mrs Simpson:	I'm not very well.
Doctor:	*(Exasperated)* Well, what are your symptoms?
Mrs Simpson:	Well Doctor... It happened last Tuesday or was it the Tuesday before. Gurpal my neighbour he knocked on my door ...
Doctor:	*(Annoyed)* That's very well, my dear Mrs Simpson, but will you please tell me. What are your symptoms?
Mrs Simpson:	Well, I can't stop blinking, I've got bendy thumbs. My arms are all wavy and a I have a wobbly bum. My legs are like jelly. My trumps are dead smelly. Oh Doctor, Doctor I'm not very well.
Doctor:	*(Sarcastically)* I know you are one of my patients but I'm slowly losing mine. Now, what are your symptoms for the very last time?
Mrs Simpson:	*(Crying)* Well, Doctor ... I woke up last Thursday. I thought I was dead. With my socks on my hands and my pants on my head.
Doctor:	*(Calmly)* Now, stop crying Mrs Simpson here is a tissue, I'm just trying to find out what are your issues.
Mrs Simpson:	Like I've been saying Doctor. I can't stop blinking; I've got bendy thumbs. My arms are all wavy and a I have a wobbly bum. My legs are like jelly. My trumps are dead smelly Oh Doctor, Doctor I'm not very well.

Doctor: Mrs Simpson, I know you don't like me and you say I'm a grump. But you've been here every day for the last twelve months. I know you leave here every day full of sorrow...

Mrs Simpson: *(Interrupts)* Oh, don't worry Doctor, same time tomorrow?

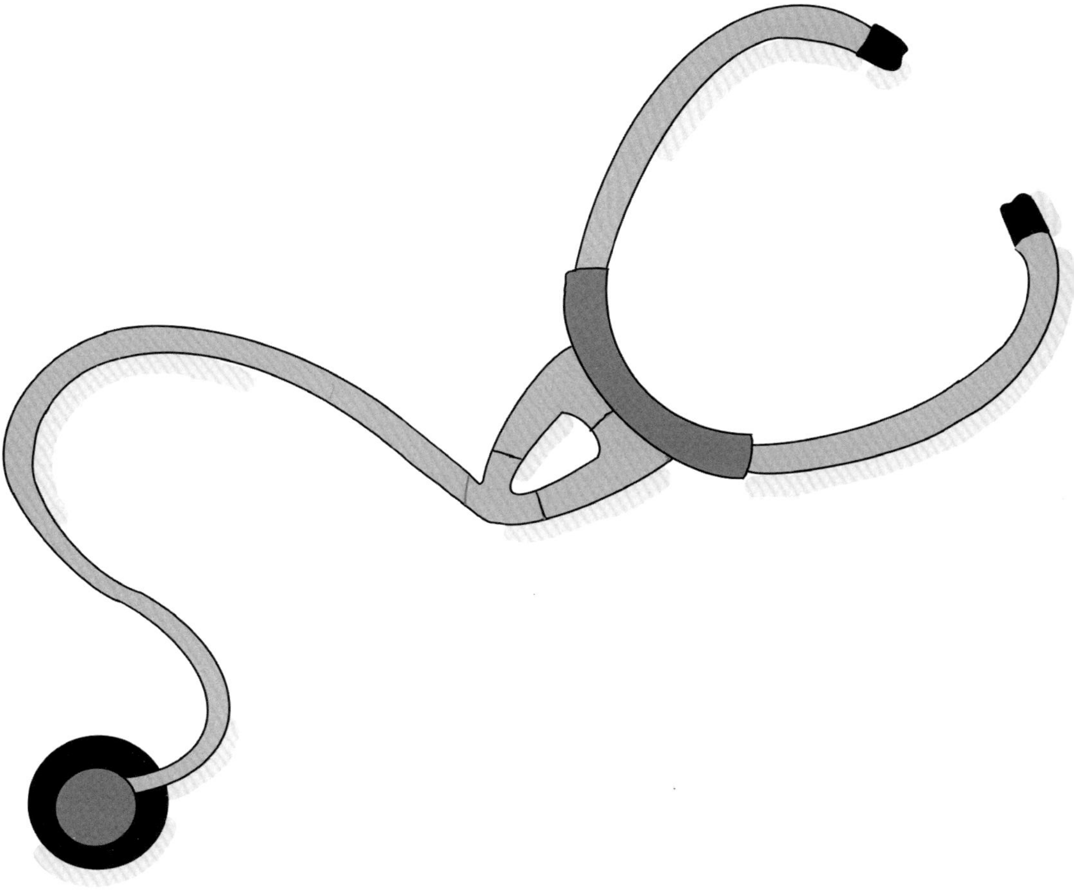

Don’t Wear a Kilt on Stilts

Never wear a kilt.
If you’re walking on stilts.
Sadly, a lesson
that I’d forgotten.

The wind it came.
There’s no one to blame.
My kilt flew up
and flashed my bottom.

Ee by Gum

Edward, my friend, asked me to write him a poem.
Everyone knows that I barely know him.
Egged along by my class, I picked up my pen.
Eager to start. Oh, but where to begin?

Excited by the idea, I began with gusto.
Effortlessly, I wrote but making no fuss though.
Elegantly, my pen moved and the ink it did flow.
Each word that I scribbled my face was aglow.

Ecstasy and excitement etched all over my face.
Enthusiastically, I wrote and the words they did race.
Embracing ideas, rhymes and notions.
Energetically, I composed Edward's new poem.

Every now and then I stared at the clock.
Empty now of ideas, I wanted to stop.
Enduring the heartache, enduring the pain.
Exasperated, I said, "Never again."

Eleven o'clock came and I was defeated.
Eyesight and energy levels, totally depleted.
Experts in poetry I hope you'll agree.
Try not to start every line with the letter E.

Goldilocks Has Lost the Plot

Goldilocks lost the plot
the day she went for a ramble.
I knew she would, go to the woods
and set a poor example.

In the early evening there in the clearing
she spied a cute little house.
She opened the door and crossed the floor,
creeping as quiet as a mouse.

She'd walked for miles and saw the piles
of books there upon a shelf.
She loved to read, she did indeed
and chose one to read to herself.

Without a care she sat on a chair
the middle one painted blue.
She had limited choices and made no noises
as she'd broken the other two.

Being selfish and feeling peckish,
she decided to look for some grub.
It lifted her soul when she saw three bowls
and porridge she really loved.

One was lumpy the other one bumpy
but one was deliciously sweet.
It was almost dawn, she began to yawn
and decided to go upstairs for a sleep.

She got to the room and lit by the moon,
were three beds of differing sizes.
One was big, one was small
and the middle one was truly delightful.

Her eyes she closed and began to doze
but was awoken by a roar from behind.
Her jaw it dropped her eyes they popped.
There were three bears, of the grizzly kind.

She was shaking inside, began to cry
She even started to beg.
She shouted "Look!' they all looked up
and she escaped between their legs.

She was off like a shot and didn't stop
Until, she was at last safe in her bed.
She said her prayers and prayed for the bears
and promised never to do that again.

Granny's Invented a Time Machine

There was a scene at my Granny's last Saturday night.
I knew straight away that things weren't right
There were Normans and Romans, Victorians galore.
Charles Dickens and Lowry having a chat by the door.

There were Cavemen in the kitchen. Vikings upstairs.
My granny and Brunel, playing musical chairs.
I called to my Gran and asked what was going on?
She smiled and replied, "Oh hello, have you come to visit me son?"

She told me all about her night school and college.
Her maths, her science, her engineering knowledge.
"Oh love, I'm so excited and so is Maureen.
We've only gone and invented a time machine."

She explained about the things that she'd found in the shed.
A few old clocks, some bolts and a wrought iron bed.
A collection of wires and a new motherboard.
A two-pin hairdryer that she'd bought from abroad.

She told me about meeting Tutankhamen.
Then Amy Winehouse who was singing some tunes.
"Dick Turpin visited but he didn't stop.
He went out for some milk and held up the shop."

"The Battle of Hastings wasn't much fun.
Poor Maureen got an arrow straight in her bum.
We've met some Romans with big hooked noses.
King Richard III from the War of the Roses."

I couldn't believe what I was seeing
All these people were alive before I was born.
I nearly died, when I looked outside.
Joan of Arc was mowing the lawn

Leaning calmly against the cooker.
Boudicca said, "Maureen we've ran out of sugar."
"Elvis love, will you pop to the shops?"
"Will do Momma, thank you very much."

"Oh, I need some biscuits, will you shout him son."
"It's too late Nan he's already gone."
Ghandi was laughing as he lay there chilling.
"Sorry my love, Elvis has left the building."

I told her, "Nan this has to stop, you must know it's wrong?
These people have to go back to where they belong."
"I know my sweet, they're all returning today
and that silly old machine, we'll throw it away."

Guess What I Saw Today?

I saw a little bee today,
hopping to and fro.
Down below I spied a worm,
wriggling really slow.

I saw a little mouse today
scuttling here and there.
Up above was a friendly frog,
flying through the air.

I saw a little fish today
swimming under water.
Another fish swam by her side
perhaps it was her daughter.

I saw a little slug today
looking rather frail.
She has no home to call her own
and dreams of being a snail.

Safely, tucked up inside his web,
today, I spied a spider.
He was watching spider football
and drinking Spider Cider!

Handy Aunty Hannah

(To be recited in a Geordie Accent)

My Auntie Hannah's
got eight hands.
Which sounds like a bit of a fuss.

She can multitask
and fend off attacks.
A bit like an octopus.

She can scramble eggs
and shave her legs.
Whilst cooking cheese on toast.

She can carefully crochet
four scarfs at once
but she doesn't like to boast.

My Auntie Hannah's got eight hands,
and she's sent from heaven above.
It's not funny, she's got no money.
As she spends it all on gloves!

Happy Families

My mum has given dad the flu
she got it at the shops.
My dad gave my little brother Max,
the gift of chickenpox.

Little Max is really cross
and is planning to run off.
But before he goes (with his snotty
nose)
my sister caught his cough.

Lucy says it doesn't bother her
she always likes to boast.
She gave our nan a sloppy kiss
and a very poorly throat.

Poor old nan is really sad
and grandad needs a hug.
Now he's gone missing, I bet he's fishing,
perhaps he'll catch a bug.

Homework Homesick Blues

I hate homework,
It's a dreadful waste of time.
The Government must ban it.
It should be deemed a crime.

It should be deemed a crime.
To make kids work at home.
My mates are all playing outside.
I have to sit on my own.

I have to sit on my own.
Calculating really hard sums.
I spend hours working them out.
Sadly, the answers won't come.

Sadly, the answers won't come.
They giggle and pretend to hide.
Instead of practising spellings.
There's part of me crying inside.

There's part of me crying inside.
Trying to name kings and queens.
Staring blankly at a French text book.
I don't know what anything means.

I don't know what anything means.
My algebra, I just don't understand.
I'm going to write to the Prime Minister.
Asking for homework to be banned.

POETRY
FEAR REFRAMED
HISTORY

Horace the Hip Hop Hoss

Clip clop, clip clop.
Are the sound of Horace's hooves.
Or clippty-clopperty-clip-clop-clip.
When he's doing his disco moves.

Horace is such a formidable force.
He's hip-hop Horace, the Hip Hop horse.

He goes outside to dance with the neighbours.
Samba, Mamba or the Macarena.
Horace moves as he knows the grooves,
With his flowing mane and his lightning hooves.

Tango, Tap, Twist and Rumba.
His hip hop hooves, sound like thunder.
Salsa, Street, the old hip-hop.
He is Horace the horse and he's so Hip Hop.

Barn dance, belly dance. He knows the lot.
His foxtrot hooves, they glow red-hot.
Disco, Calypso and he likes a bit of Latin.
Dancing's in his blood. It's his passion

Horace is such a formidable force.
He's hip-hop Horace, the Hip Hop horse.

Some horses like the dressage and prancing.
Not our Horace. He's loves breakdancing.
He can floss like a boss and body pop too.
Loves a bit a ballet and can pirouette too.

Tango, Tap, Twist and Rumba.
His hip hop hooves, sound like thunder.
Salsa, Street, the old hip-hop.
He is Horace the horse and he's so Hip Hop.

Jitterbug, Jive and the Mash Potato.
He's bowing out now and he'll see y'all later

Horace is such a formidable force.
He's hip-hop Horace, the Hip Hop horse.

Who is he?

He's hip-hop Horace, the Hip Hop horse.

One more time.

He's hip-hop Horace, the Hip Hop horse.

I've Got an Itch

I've got an itch,
nothing drastic.
I really, really
need to scratch it.
I'll get a coat hanger
made from plastic.
Oh, that's better.
That feels fantastic.
Scratch. Scratch. Scratch.

I've got an itch.
I'm not being dramatic.
I really, really
need to scratch it.
I'll get a spatula
made from plastic.
Oh, that's better.
I feel ecstatic.
Scratch. Scratch. Scratch

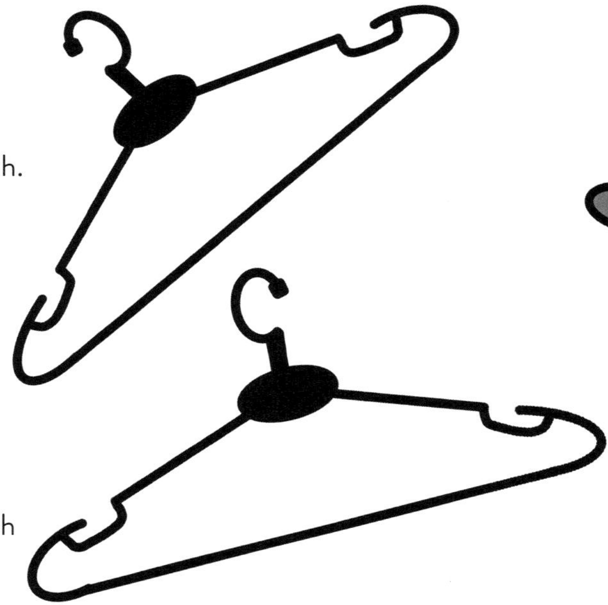

I Am Grateful

I am grateful, for the wind that blows.
I am grateful, for my wiggly toes.
I am grateful, for the rain that falls.
I am grateful, for the bug that crawls.

I am grateful, for the falling snow.
I am grateful, for my nose that glows.
I am grateful, for the misty fog.
I am grateful, for you, my God.

I am grateful, for the bright sunshine.
I am grateful that you are mine.

I'm in Heaven with FD 1.1.11

There's a girl I know,
That I love lots.
There's only one problem,
I've heard she's a robot.

We've only just met
and I barely know her.
A friend told me that
her name is Fiona.

She has rosy red cheeks,
just like a geranium.
She's made of steel, rubber
and a touch of titanium.

She has aluminium eyelashes
and her bottom is carbon.
Whenever she trumps,
she always says pardon.

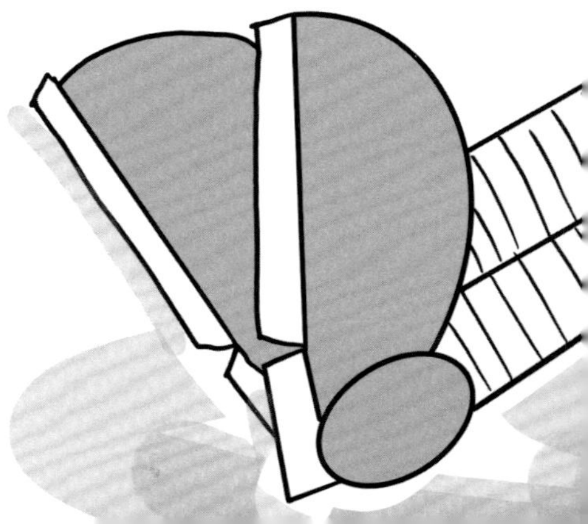

FE
FD1.1.11

I'm the Head and I'm in Charge!

Let's calm down and sit up straight.
Oi you! Stop talking to your mate.
Let's all stay in our own little rows.
Oi you! With your finger up your nose.
Good morning, I'm Mr Clark.
I'm the Head and I'm in charge!
Who am I?
(You're the Head and you're in charge.)
Once again?
(You're the Head and you're in charge.)

Welcome back to a brand new term.
Willie! Get up son, you're a boy not a worm.
I would like to remind you about our uniforms.
Plain white shirt, no unicorns!
We all know that peacocks are funky.
Put on your blazer you cheeky little monkey.

I'm glad that I've got you all together.
You're a girl not a chicken, sit down Heather.
Johnny's much better, you'll be glad to hear.
Eating conkers was a bad idea.
Quiet now - it's your very last chance.
Oi Peter, have you got ants in your pants?

Let's calm down and sit up straight.
Oi you! Stop talking to your mate.
Let's all stay in our own little rows.
Oi you! With your finger up your nose.
Good morning, I'm Mr Clark.
I'm the Head and I'm in charge!
Who am I?
(You're the Head and you're in charge.)
Once again?
(You're the Head and you're in charge.)

Now for the news. I need listening ears.
How do I know if penguins have ears?
Dinner was lovely, I hope you'll agree.
Remember Quentin has a nut allergy.
Thank you, Mrs Jones for your lovely cooking.
Coxy! chocolate bars aren't classed as a pudding.

Our school motto is 'LOVE ONE ANOTHER.'
Karl! Pencil down. You're not a conductor.
Nancy deserves a great big clap.
She's written a poem called the Scarecrow Rap.
I've had a letter from Ryan's mum.
He can't join in as he can't wiggle his bum.

Let's calm down and sit up straight.
Oi you! Stop talking to your mate.
Let's all stay in our own little rows.
Oi you! With your finger up your nose.
Good morning, I'm Mr Clark.
I'm the Head and I'm in charge!
Who am I?
(You're the Head and you're in charge.)
Once again?
(You're the Head and you're in charge.)

Oi, Gum out. Put it in the bin.
How do you know my real name's Tim?
Cassie has won another karate trophy.
This is Harvey our new school goalie,
We're not doing anymore clay work or pottery.
It's been cancelled since Miss won the lottery.

Our star this week is Head Boy Kevin.
How do I know if pens go to heaven?
Kathleen's proud that her hair is ginger.
But Mike stop calling her a whinging ninja.
What's the best thing about my job?
Teaching all you little Crocodilla-Hollapogs!

Let's calm down and sit up straight.
Oi you! Stop talking to your mate.
Let's all stay in our own little rows.
Oi you! With your finger up your nose.
Good morning, I'm Mr Clark.
I'm the Head and I'm in charge!
Who am I?
(You're the Head and you're in charge.)
Once again?
(You're the Head and you're in charge.)

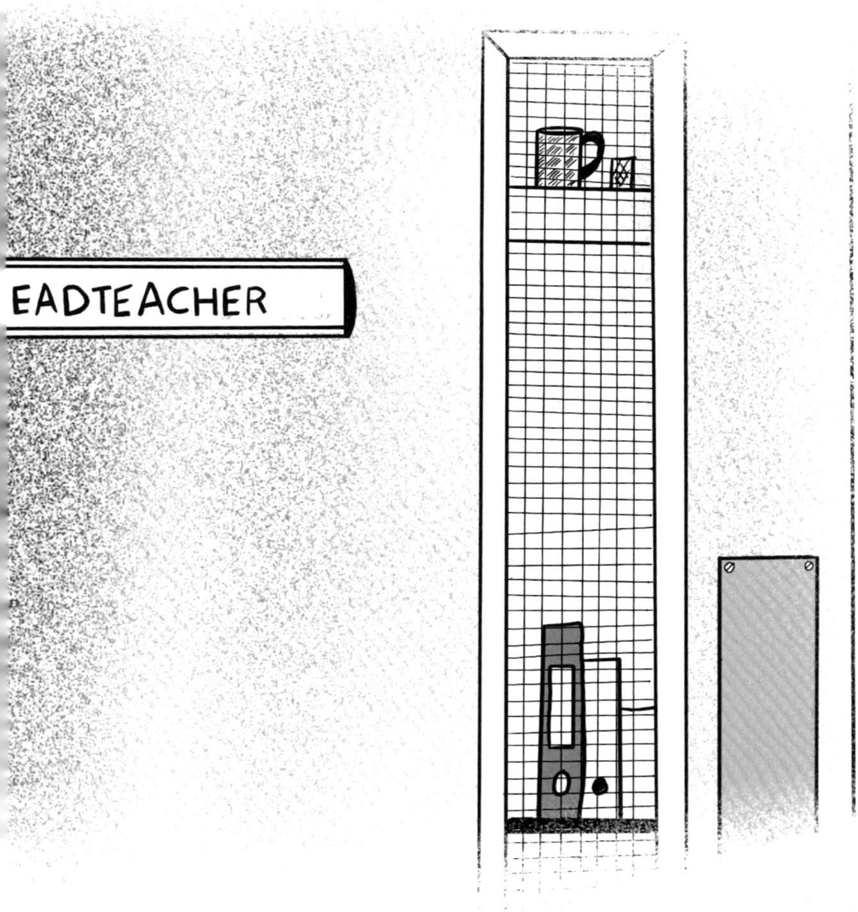
EADTEACHER

If I Were ...

If I were a dog, I'd wag my little tail.
I'd move really slow if I were a snail.

If I were a cheetah, I'd run really fast.
I'd hang upside down if I were a bat.

If I were a cockerel, I'd shout, "Cock-A-Doodle-Doo."
I'd jump really high if I were a kangaroo.

If I were a Polar bear, I'd stay warm in a blizzard.
I'd catch flies on my tongue if I were a lizard.

If I were a dolphin, I'd make my tail swish.
I'd call everyone 'Bob' if I were a fish.

If I were a flamingo, I'd stand a little wonky.
I'd call "Hee-Haw" if I were a donkey.

If I were a chicken, I'd strut around in circles.
I'd pop my head out my shell if I were a turtle.

If I were a horse, I'd proudly wear my saddle.
I'd drink lots of water if I were a camel.

If I were an owl, I'd have a little nap,
I‘d move from side to side if I were a crab.

If I were an elephant I'd wave with my trunk.
I'd really, really pong if I were a skunk.

I've given it lots of thought and I hope you'll agree.
I'm really, really happy just being me.

I Just Want to be a Plumber

When I was young the teacher asked,
What did we want to be?
I put my hand up, straight away.
“Sir, Sir, pick me!”

I don’t want to be an actor,
or a star of the stage and screen
or a grumpy goth with a linen cloth
who has to clean, clean, clean.

I don’t want to be a pop star
or a really famous drummer.
I just wanna be, I just wanna be,
I just wanna be a plumber.

Playing with pipes is my only dream.
It has been, most of my life.
I couldn’t cope with an office job
with all that trouble and strife.

I don’t want to be a locksmith
who deals with locks and keys.
I’m a nice chappie an’ I’m really
happy,
dealing with poos and wees.

I don’t want to be an athlete
or even a long-distance runner.
I just wanna be, I just wanna be
I just wanna be a plumber.

I don’t want to be a baker,
a builder or a nurse
or the chap with the cap,
who drives a big black hearse.

Fitting sinks and soldering joints,
would fill my heart with pride
or taking off the cistern lid
and having a look inside.

I don’t want to be a lifeguard
working right through the summer.
I just wanna be, I just wanna be
I just wanna be a plumber.

I just want to unblock toilets,
that’s all I want to do.
To get my spanner, saw and hammer
and flush away the poo.

I don’t want to be a dentist
who deals with crowns and molars
or the shady, old man in the big white
van,
selling kettles and toasters.

I can’t wait to leave this place,
Is it any wonder?
I just wanna be, I just wanna be
I just wanna be a plumber.

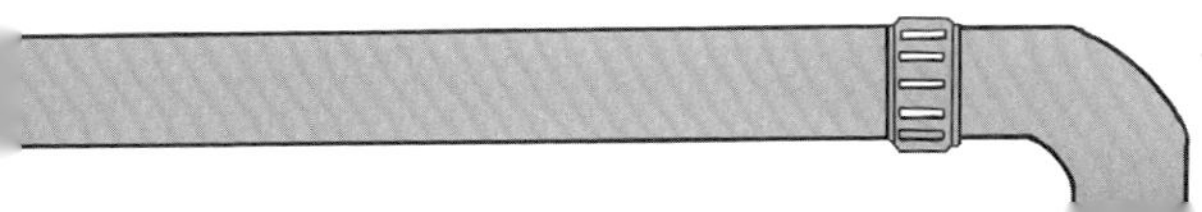

I Love Ruby Russell

I think I'm in love.
My legs are all trembly.
I sat behind her
today in morning assembly.

That bright red ribbon
in her long blonde hair.
She stares right through me
as if I'm not there.

The rules of love,
to me are a puzzle.
Don't tell anyone
I'm in love with Ruby Russell.

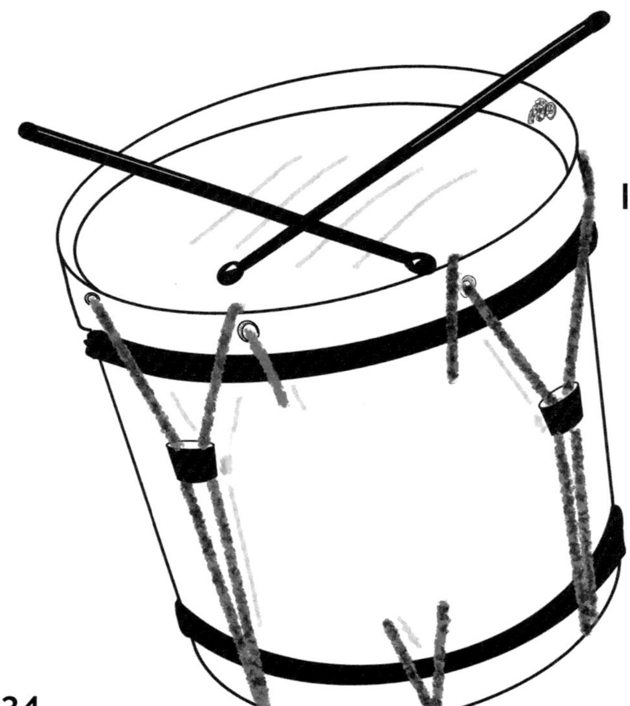

Imogen Crumbs

Imogen Crumbs
played the drums.
Her sister played the bass.
Her brother Billy
was very silly.
He just played his face.

I Should Have Been a Superhero

I could've been a super hero
but I'm really scared of heights.
I think I'd look dead stupid
with my pants outside my tights

Anyway, I hate the feel of Lycra
and masks they itch my face.
In the world of superheroes
I'd be a huge disgrace.

My climbing is atrocious
my running's even worse.
Instead of fighting baddies
I'd rather see a nurse.

I'm petrified of rats and bats
and spiders make me heave.
I wouldn't have a trendy name.
I'd just be... Super Steve.

That's why I'm not a superhero
with matching boots and cape.
Instead of fighting crooks and thugs.
I'd prefer some tea and cake.

It's 'Orrible Looking For Love When You're a Shark

(To be recited in a West Country accent)

I went on a date
with skate named Kate.
She turned pale grey
when she saw me.
No love at first sight,
she screamed with fright.
Then just tried her best
to ignore me.

It's 'orrible looking for love when you're a shark.
For I always end up with a broken heart.
I just want a partner for the here ever after.
It's 'orrible looking for love.
It's 'orrible looking for love.
It's 'orrible looking for love.
When you're a shark.

I swim around every day,
all over the old sea bed.
When I meet a friend, they just pretend.
They're asleep or even dead.
It's a lonely life without a wife,
I'm full of sadness and grief.
It's really tough looking for love
as they faint when they see my teeth.

It's 'orrible looking for love when you're a shark.
For I always end up with a broken heart.
I just want a partner for the here ever after.
It's 'orrible looking for love.
It's 'orrible looking for love.
It's 'orrible looking for love.
When you're a shark.

Jane Frost

Oh, look at me. I'm the boss.
Prince of Snow and King of the Frost.
There's no rhyme, reason or riddle,
He'll cover your garden in sugar crystals.

Forget your baubles, tinsel and glitter.
I'm Jealous Jane, Jack Frost's sister.
It should be Miss Frost instead of Mr.
I'm Jealous Jane, Jack Frost's sister.

He's hard to forget but easy to remember.
He pops his head up in early November
and turns our paths, into slippy ice rinks.
He gets on my nerves. I think he stinks.

Forget your baubles, tinsel and glitter.
I'm Jealous Jane, Jack Frost's sister.
It should be Miss Frost instead of Mr.
I'm Jealous Jane, Jack Frost's sister.

He's Jack Frost, your winter's dream.
He turns your breath into clouds of steam.
He'll freeze your nose until it glows.
Frostbite your fingers and your poor little toes.

Forget your baubles, tinsel and glitter.
I'm Jealous Jane, Jack Frost's sister.
It should be Miss Frost instead of Mr.
I'm Jealous Jane, Jack Frost's sister.

Being the youngest is a bit of a curse,
I'd be in charge, if I'd been first.
Some people say I'm a little vain.
But instead of Jack frost, you'd worship Jane.

Forget your baubles, tinsel and glitter.
I'm Jealous Jane, Jack Frost's sister.
It should be Miss Frost instead of Mr.
I'm Jealous Jane, Jack Frost's sister.

Jigsaw Pieces

Like the best dream I've ever had.
You're the one that makes me glad.
Glad to be alive and full of fun.
Like a laser gun, you're spot on.
On the money and in my head.
Like the comfort of my bed.
You're the one that keeps me sane.
Holds my hand and calls me names.
Like "Honey bunch" or "Buttercup."
When I'm down, you pick me up.
Like a brand new, shiny pick-up truck.
I like you and you like me.
Like jigsaw pieces, we fit perfectly.

Like jigsaw pieces, I like your curves.
You're in my mind and get on my nerves.
Like those who say, "I'll see you later!"
Or like a really slow, airport escalator.
You're the best film I've ever seen.
Like a queen of the screen, a dream.
A beautiful dream. Nothing scary.
Unlike my aunty Mary, who works in the vets,
where we first met. You sat there all alone.
Like a poorly pet, who hadn't been collected.
Yet, I knew then that I'd love you forever.
Like jigsaw pieces, we fit together.

Katie P – Our Brand New Striker

The Dog and Doublet
have a brand-new striker.
Her name is Katie P
and there's no one like her.

She will play in the summer
or when it's freezing.
She can score with both feet,
about thirty a season.

Scissor kicks and volleys,
she can score the lot.
Her dribbling is sublime
her boots glow red hot.

Katie can kick a ball
as fast as a rocket.
She eats defenders for breakfast
like snacks in her pocket.

The opposition fear her.
She heads the ball like a bullet.
She's the jewel in the crown
of The Dog and Doublet.

The crowd they all sing...

"Katie P, Katie P, Katie P, Katie P..." and fade.

Limericks

Gus the Poet

There was a young man called Gus.
He used to write rhymes in a rush.
He ventured to Brighton.
But forgot how to write 'em.
So, he just travelled back home on the bus.

Dolly's Off her Trolley.

There was a young lady called Dolly.
Who had a liking for mayhem and folly.
Poor Doctor McMillan,
Then gave her opinion.
Saying that Dolly was right of her trolley.

Looking in the Mirror.

I look in the mirror.
I see my face.
I think to myself,
I look ace.

I look in the mirror
I love to pose
I have two lovely eyes
and a cute little nose.

I look in the mirror
I don't really care.
I think to myself
I love your hair.

I look in the Mirror
I love what I see.
I see a beautiful reflection.
I think that's me!

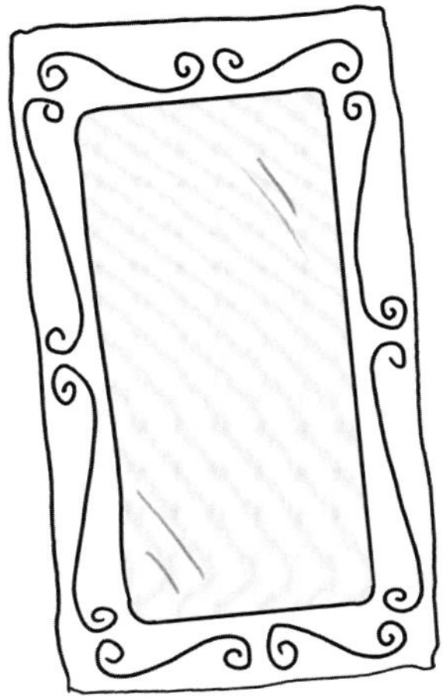

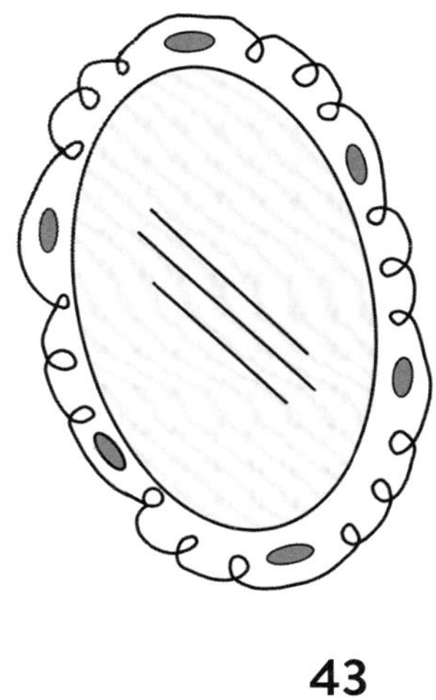

Luck of the Drawer

Characters:

Spoon: Happy, joyous and carefree, sees the good in everyone and everything.
Knife: Bitter and twisted, very cutting and is usually nasty to everyone.
Fork: Sad and dejected (was once happy) he is married to knife.
Potato Peeler: Confident and a little brash. Likes to brag a little.
Corkscrew: Very posh, well-to-do and politely spoken. Doesn't like any of the other cutlery.

The Setting:

Inside a cutlery draw in a very modern, stylish kitchen and the owner of the house has just closed the kitchen drawer.

Narrator: They turned off the lights and closed the door. Suddenly, whispers could be heard from the kitchen drawer.

Spoon: *(Joyfully)* Oh, how happy and lucky are we, to have the title of cutlery? We couldn't really ask for more, we even have our very own drawer.

Knife: *(Angrily)* Oh shut up spoon! Give it a rest. Do you realise that we're far from blessed.

Spoon: Be a nice Knifey, my sweet, no more cutting remarks.

Fork: *(Miserable)* How can you be so happy? We're all stuck here in the dark!

Spoon: *(Laughing)* Oh Freddie Fork, don't look so glum.

Knife: *(Nastily)* Don't listen to her, she's a pain in the bum.

Spoon: *(Smiling with her arms wide open)* Our hearts should be full as we're the winners, each day we're used for breakfast, lunch and dinner.

Knife: *(Sarcastically)* Spoon you're a loon. That's not the worst, you're dipped into coffee each morning, head first.

Fork: *(Sounding crestfallen and forlorn)* Spoon, we all know that you love your life. But try being married to my wife Knife. She's sharp, she's cutting, she's too hot to handle.

Spoon: *(Lovingly smiling)* But that is love my friend and love is a gamble.

Knife: *(Between gritted teeth)* Does she ever stop with this incessant ramble?

Spoon: Oh, Knifey, Knifey. I can mend your bitter heart. My dearest friend, I am a healer. Have you met my partner Potato Peeler?

Peeler: *(Rather smug in a Geordie Accent)* Alright knife, ye miserable toad! What's th' matter wi' you. Are you getting old? Life for you just isn't good. As I'm far better at peeling spuds. Aye, carrots, parsnips I can peel the lot. You're just bitter cos' I've took yer job.

Fork: *(Trying to be brave but he's petrified inside)* Peeler that's enough! Don't you ever speak to my wife like that! *(He lifts his arm to hold back his wife)* It's okay, I'll deal with this Pat.

Knife: *(Pushes her husband's arm away and darts towards Peeler.)* Fork you're a dork, get out of my way. Come here peeler, what did you say?

Spoon: *(Trying to remain positive)* Come on, come on, let's not fight. I've got some games planned for tonight. Whisk says that she'll be here later, she's out on a date with the new cheese grater.

Corkscrew: *(Very posh and looks down on the rest)* Don't include me, I'll be fine. Anyway, I'm going out later as they've bought some wine.

Fork: What about fish slice have you spoken to him?

Knife: Nah, he's out with that contraption that opens tins.

Spoon: *(Looking perplexed)* What's that noise? Can you hear that humming? Right! Back to your places there's someone coming.

Many

Many run because they're late.
Many cry outside the gate.
Many laugh and push each other.
Many are bullied by their brothers.
Many dawdle and drag their bag.
Many boast, embellish or brag.
Many gather and talk out loud.
Many have their head within the clouds.
Many are worried about their maths.
Many have showers instead of baths.
Many are young and many are older.
Many just wish that the day was over.

This is Monday, I'm one of the flock.
I'm in the playground and it's 9 o'clock.

Monday is Not a Fun Day.

Monday's not a fun day.
It's the day I go to school.
Tuesday, she makes me go again.
My mum's just being cruel.
Dad calls Wednesday 'Hump Day'
as he relaxes with a beer.
Thursday is a good day.
The weekend's almost here.
It's Friday, school's over, I shout a loud, 'Yipee.'
I'm on my way to Granny's and she said it's chippy tea.

Noah's Long List

The animals started to clamber aboard,
this made Old Noah smile.
Mrs. Noah, looking rather perplexed grumbled,
"Is this going to take a while?"

Noah ignored the moans of his wife,
ticking off animals, two by two.
Two baboons, two raccoons,
then a rather shy kangaroo.

"Oh, I'm so sorry Noah, my love."
came the pleas from the kangaroo.
"We've both had too many coffees
and my husband's popped to the loo!"

The stern face gorillas climbed aboard,
carrying the jellyfish, safe in a tank.
"Morning Noah," smiled Paula the Penguin.
"Have you met my husband, Frank?"

Next, were the octopuses, with their sixteen cases,
trying to hide their cunning deception.
The owls were unhappy about the Wi-Fi
and complained of the poor connection.

Noah smiled as he ticked them all off,
counting flippers, horns and beaks.
Barry the snail arrived at the end of the plank,
which he'd been crawling for two and a half weeks.

The funky peacock was full of questions,
"Is there a pool or a spa?"
Koalas and pandas were wildly dancing,
as the chimp, he strummed his guitar.

The spiders were all tangled in cobwebs
the slugs covering everything in slime.
The ostrich asked Noah for a selfie,
whilst the zebras, they marched in a line.

The badgers, the bats and the aardvarks.
Stood there, trembling with fright.
"Mr Noah, you do know, we're all nocturnal
and we only come out at night?"

Two flaming flamingos both flew in,
wearing pink boots and cowboy hats.
Joined by two angry alligators,
adorning t-shirts emblazoned with cats.

The chameleons were confusing poor Noah,
changing colours ever so quick.
As quick as a flash, on board they did dash.
Instead of two, there were six.

The parrots squawked in unison,
shaking the odd tail-feather.
The free-range hen clucked, "I don't live in a pen
and you can call me Heather."

"Can you show me the way to the duty free?"
was the request of the worm called Willie.
"I'd like to buy my wife a birthday gift.
If I forget, she'll surely kill me!"

"Row, row, row your boat!"
Came the slurs of the poodles, Julie & Terry.
"Oh Julie, I'm going to be sick overboard,
we shouldn't have drunk that sherry."

"Excuse me, young man. Are you in charge?"
Enquired Donna the ditzy dingo.
"I can't find the cinema anywhere
and what about the disco and bingo?"

"Can anyone show me the way to the gym?"
Questioned Ryan, the muscly red panda.
"Oh, flipping heck, have you seen his pecks?"
The goose shouted, "Go on give us a gander."

The sharks, the whales and the dolphins,
asked Noah, if they could swim alongside.
"We'll swim whilst we natter and if we are shattered,
we'll just jump onboard for the ride."

The moose, the goose and the turkey cock,
were playing badminton up on the deck.
Allowing, Tina the rock-hard robin,
to keep all the birdies in check.

Leo the lion strolled around,
pretending he owned the place.
He let out a roar and collapsed on the floor,
when the seagull pooped in his face.

The nightingales they started a choir,
singing songs and taking requests.
Colin the crow was the official look-out,
Snuggled up there in his nest.

The turtle doves arrived in time,
just as Noah was closing the door.
At last, the animals were safe in the arc,
with not a single soul on the shore.

On it Like a Bard's Sonnet

Young sprightly Bill from yonder, Stratford way.
Johnny Shakespeare's lad, I've heard them say.
The boy is so nimble with mind and quill.
He writes plays and poems does our lad Bill.

He's a handsome man with a goodly face.
Loves a bit of satin, velvet and lace.
He's balding on top, he's losing his thatch.
But his beautiful beard makes up for that.

Bill's love life, alas was a lottery.
He tried his luck down there in Shottery.
The charming Anne Hathaway, Bill found there.
She was sprightly, brightly, both bonnie and fare.

Bill said, "Read my poems, your heart will fly.
In four hundred years, they'll make school kids cry."

On Me Holibobs!

(To be recited in your best Lancashire accent)

The summer's here, we're out of school
The weather's warm so we'll play it cool.
No more homework, no more jobs.
We're all off on our holibobs.
We're all off on our holibobs.

Heading off to Wales or the coast of Devon
or sitting in your pants till half past eleven.
Staying up late and bouncing on my bed.
Then in the morning pretending I'm dead.
Dragged by my gran around the local shops.
That's what I did on my six weeks off.

The summer's here, we're out of school
The weather's warm so we'll play it cool.
No more homework, no more jobs.
We're all off on our holibobs.
We're all off on our holibobs.

Sweets, treats and homemade pancakes.
Midnight feasts under the blankets.
Shaking with fright under the covers.
Being told ghost stories by your big bad brother.
Running round crazy after drinking blue pop.
That's what I did on my six weeks off.

The summer's here, we're out of school
The weather's warm so we'll play it cool.
No more homework, no more jobs.
We're all off on our holibobs.
We're all off on our holibobs.

Days were carefree, no worries insight.
Fresh summer mornings and long warm nights.

They say that all good things must come to an end.
It's September next week, I was told by a friend.
But I can't go to school as I have a nasty cough.
I'll just tell my mum I need another six weeks off.

The summer's here, we're out of school
The weather's warm so we'll play it cool.
No more homework, no more jobs.
We're all off on our holibobs.
We're all off on our holibobs.

Otto Signs for United

I've seen the news and I'm so excited.
Otto the Ostrich has signed for United.
The manager said there's only one reason.
Otto will bag us forty goals in a season.
The 'Wizard of the Wing' is what they call him.
Send in a cross and he'll head the ball in.

Instead of chanting 'Here We Go.'
The crowd all sing ...
Ostrich O, Ostrich O, Ostrich O,
Ostrich O, Ostrich O, Ostrich O-Oh

We were worried that the deal was over.
That Otto had signed for Barcelona.
Getting Otto was a stroke of luck.
He's gonna win us the FA Cup.
Some players use the old nutmeg.
But Otto just blinks and lays an egg.

Instead of chanting 'Here We Go.'
The crowd all sing ...
Ostrich O, Ostrich O, Ostrich O,
Ostrich O, Ostrich O, Ostrich O-Oh

I'm sad for the others, it's such a pity.
The likes of the Wanderers, Albion and of couse City.
Otto's fast he can dribble and tackle.
He can score with both, it doesn't matter.
At 3pm on Saturday he'll steal the show.
In his bright red shirt that says Ostrich O.

Instead of chanting 'Here We Go.'
The crowd all sing ...
Ostrich O, Ostrich O, Ostrich O,
Ostrich O, Ostrich O, Ostrich O-Oh

Pirate Problems

(To recited in your best pirate accent)

"Aaaarrrrgggghhhh!" shouts the captain each day on the deck.
With his swashbuckling beard, he's a pain in the neck.
Long John Tin Leg, that's his name.
Looting's his life and plunder his game.
He shouts, he bawls, he raves and rants.
I'd like to kick him square in the ... ankle.

Hoist the mizzen, batten the hatches.
With this toing and froing,
I'll be as sick as a parrot.
*'Bluurrrrghhhh!'
Shiver-me-timbers, I'm knocking my knees.
I'm just an old pirate who's scared of the sea.

They shout, "All aboard!" and "Come on me hearties."
They promised me treasure and a life of parties.
I really never really signed up for this,
to be sick every day off the back of a ship.
Each night they give us a barrel of rum.
I drink so much I fall on my ... bed.

Hoist the mizzen, batten the hatches.
With this toing and froing,
I'll be as sick as a parrot.
*'Bluurrrrghhhh!'
Shiver-me-timbers, I'm knocking my knees.
I'm just an old pirate who's scared of the sea.

"Get up you blaggards!" the captain screams.
No time to sleep, no time to dream.
Life is so hard on the open seas.
This pirating life just isn't for me.
We scrub the decks and play the part.
Life's so busy there's no time to ... rest.

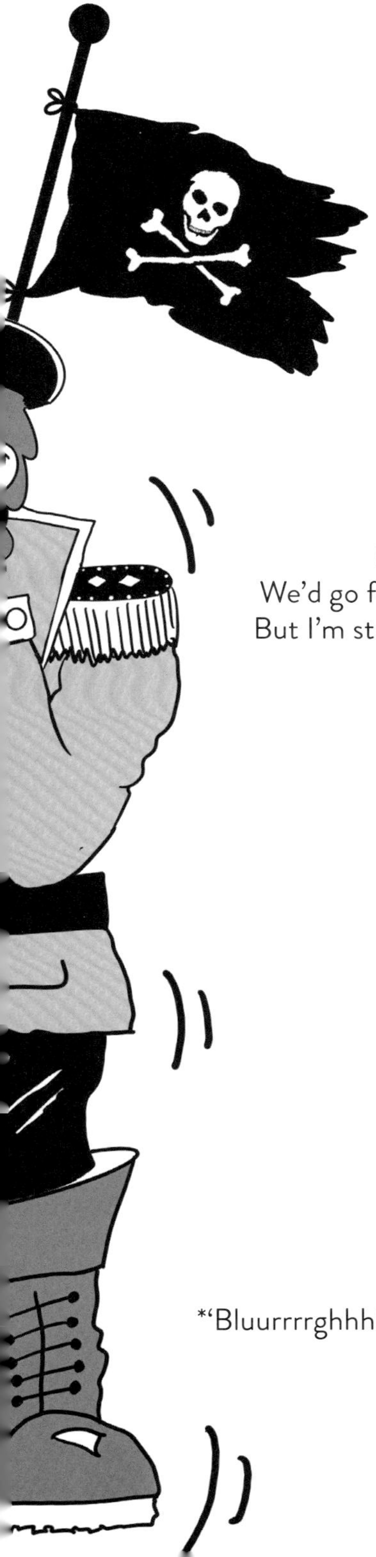

Hoist the mizzen, batten the hatches.
With this toing and froing,
I'll be as sick as a parrot.
*'Bluurrrrghhhh!'
Shiver-me-timbers, I'm knocking my knees.
I'm just an old pirate who's scared of the sea.

I wish I was home. I'd be a baker instead.
I wouldn't have seagulls poop on me head.
I'd have a lovely wife and I'd bake her fresh pastries.
We'd go for walks in the meadow and I'd pick her wild daisies.
But I'm stuck in this crow's nest and I'm frozen right through.
I need to climb down as I'm dying for a ... hot drink.

Hoist the mizzen, batten the hatches.
With this toing and froing,
I'll be as sick as a parrot.
*'Bluurrrrghhhh!'
Shiver-me-timbers, I'm knocking my knees.
I'm just an old pirate who's scared of the sea.

Shiver-me-timbers and knock my knees.
I'm just an old pirate who's scared of the sea.
I'm just an old pirate who's scared of the sea.
I'm just an old pirate who's scared of the sea.
"Aaaarrrrggggghhhh!"

A Top Pirate Tip:

*'Bluurrrrghhhh!' (Is the noise you make when you are being sick.)

Pizza Toppings

Whenever I go shopping.
I like to think of pizza toppings.
When I start there ain't no stopping.
I consider my choices, let's say, jaw dropping.

Forget your ham and pineapple rings.
I like to include more sinister things.
Pepperoni is not my favourite choice
or any of the things that people enjoy.

I like to go on a food adventure.
I slice my pizza with Granny's dentures.
I'm rather courageous I suppose.
I pick fresh bogies from up my nose.

I like a fresh slice of barbecue chicken.
Then a tiny sprinkle of dad's nail clippings.
Furballs coughed up by next door's cat
and a big dollop of fresh cow pat.

Wooden splinters and ground up charcoal.
Matted hair from down the plughole.
Mouldy old nuts from mum's bird feeder
and the contents of my vacuum cleaner.

Spicy chillies that are really, really hot.
Coughed up phlegm and a jar of snot.
Fresh strawberries and some cotton candy
and the contents of the baby's nappy.

I don't use tomato sauce. I'm a little bit snobbish.
I cover my pizza with red shoe polish.
I like old plasters. The dirtier the better.
Spiky cactus from the garden centre.

I'm only joking, I don't like any of these.
I'm really boring I just have cheese.

Poetry Aerobics

Stand up, nod your head, stick out your tongue.
Hands on your knees and wiggle your bum.
Sit down, arms up, now touch your little nose.
Straighten your legs and wiggle your toes.

Stand up, stretch tall, stick out your tongue.
Hands on your head and wiggle your bum.
Jump up, shout, "Yes," land on the ground.
Slowly and quietly, please sit down.

Stand up, balance, stick out your tongue.
Hands on your hips and wiggle your bum.
Stretch like a starfish, all alone on a beach.
Now bend over and touch your smelly feet.

Stand up, clap hands and stick out your tongue.
Pretend you're a dinosaur and wiggle your bum.
Stretch high, sit down and stand up once more.
Turn around twice and finally, sit on the floor.

Potatoes

Potatoes are so flexible
they can do most anything.
You can mash them and bash them
or boil them ‘til they sing.

You can turn them into crisps
and place them in a basket.
Or scrub them up so they look good
and serve them in their jackets.

Some people call a potato, a spud.
Whilst others call it a tater.
You can wave them goodbye in a shepherd’s pie
and shout, ‘I’ll see you later!’

You can put them in a potato salad
or turn them into fries.
But don’t leave them in the dark too long.
Or green shoots will grow from their eyes.

Life’s not good for a humble spud.
As they are roasted, boiled or fried.
So, be as kind to a spud as you can be
as each one is crying inside.

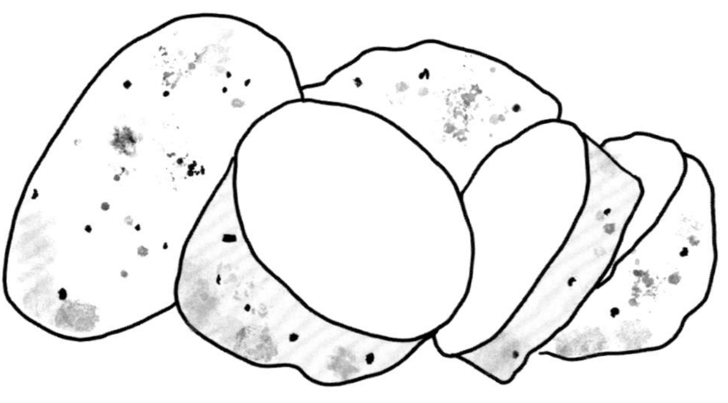

Rebecca Decker

Rebecca Decker was a wild woodpecker,
she pecked like there was no tomorrow.
She pecked so hard that her beak fell off
and it left her full of sorrow.

She flew to the doctor with her beak under her wing
Crying, “Oh Doctor, what can I do?”
But Doctor Proctor had a lot to offer
and he stuck it back on with glue.

Now Rebecca Decker has a brand-new pecker.
She is grateful for Doctor Proctor.
Every morning she heeds his warning
and she pecks just that little bit softer.

Sandra the Salamander

I'm Sandra the salamander,
I spend most of my time on a rock.
I sit in the sun, tanning my bum.
I should really be wearing my frock.

I'm a salamander and there's nothing grander,
than catching flies on my tongue.
My tail it dangles, my limbs are right angles.
If you call me a lizard, you're wrong.

My sister Brenda is long and slender,
a salamander with glamour and grace.
She's young and single, ready to mingle
and has the most beautiful face.

Scarlett's Magic Carpet

My mate Scarlett has a magic carpet,
which gives her superpowers.
I tell you man she's as fast as a tram,
and as strong as Blackpool Tower.

Now Scarlett's carpet is truly magic.
She flies around both night and day.
From Fleetwood sands to Lytham St Annes
and as far as Morecambe Bay.

Scarlett's target is to use her carpet.
The excitement it never stops.
Except when she's tired, she rolls up inside.
Like a stick of Blackpool rock.

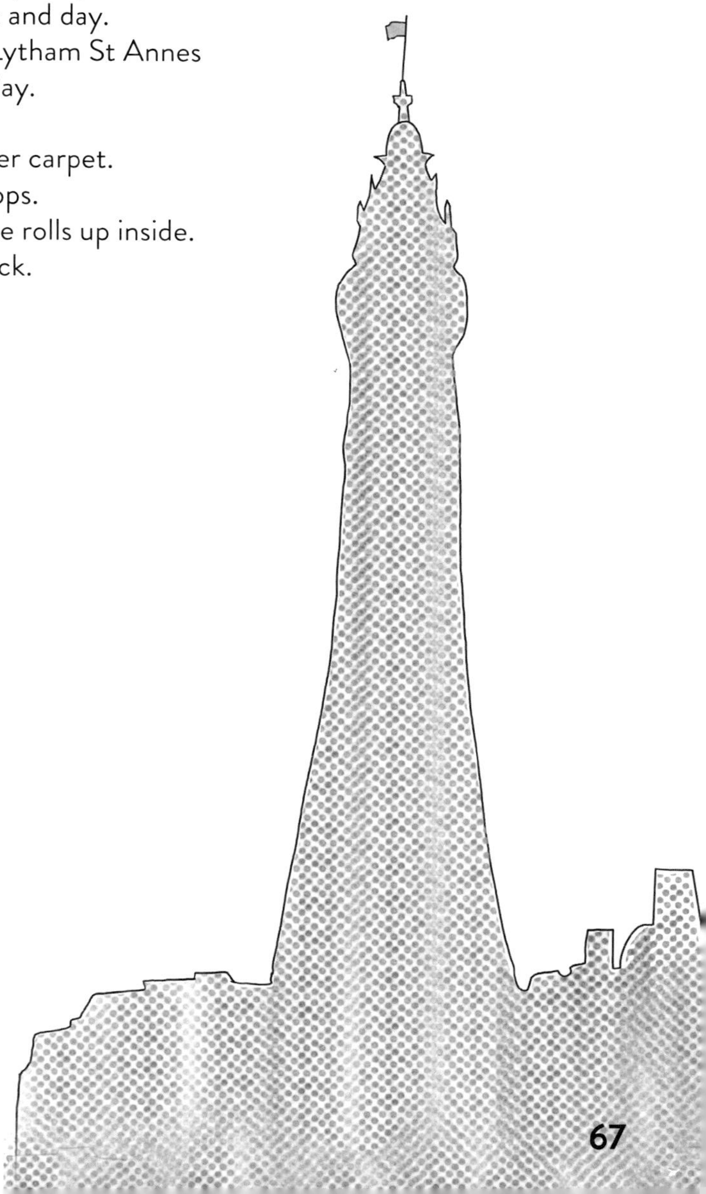

Thank You

Thank you for my dad.
Thank you for my mum.
Thank you for my ears
and my sticky out tongue.

Thank you for my smile.
Thank you for the fun.
Thank you for my fingers
and my bendy little thumb.

Thank you for my shoulders.
Thank you for my tum.
Thank you for my hips
and my wiggly little bum.

Thank you!
Thank you!
Thank you!
Thank you!

The Factory Where Teachers Are Made

Down by the canal there's a factory.
I've never been in there, I'm afraid.
It's a dark and dismal, despicable place.
I believe it's where teachers are made.

I've heard that it's in full production.
How I wish it was empty instead.
The machines roar twenty-four hours a day.
Making principals and deputy heads.

The tall Victorian chimneys.
Spew thick smoke right up into the sky.
I can't even imagine how it looks inside.
If I entered, I think I would die.

The arms, the legs and the torsos,
are delivered by vans during the day.
Highly skilled, talented artisans,
carve the heads from granite and clay.

The eyes are the next thing fitted
by a ghoul by the name of Hector.
Just there by the stairs, the eyes are in pairs.
The colder, the sinister the better.

The Hair and the Wig Departments
are run by a lady called Smith.
She makes all her wigs so realistic,
including split ends, bald patches and nits.

Paula designs all the outfits and clothes.
But likes to drink pints of beer on the bounce.
Just before noon, she's as drunk as a loon.
Sending out teachers looking like clowns.

Madame Weetman installs all the voices.
Adjusting the volume with a miniature wrench.
Some voices are deep, others are high.
Some can even talk French.

The Training Department is next.
It's the job that pays the best money.
The teachers are taught how to walk and to talk
and tell jokes that simply aren't funny.

The brain station fills them with knowledge.
It's where their brains are repaired.
The boring ones have algebra added
and the phrase, "Pi r squared.'

The teachers that are responsible for English
are programmed by a boffin called Guy.
Deep inside he hides some humour
and gives them a glint in their eye.

Alicia is there with her artistic flair.
Adding last minute details, I suppose.
She adds coffee breath, grubby nails
and dirty great hairs up their nose.

Miss Maguire works in Quality Control,
here the teachers are finally inspected.
They all have to look horrid and scary.
The kind ones are sadly rejected.

I can't ever see this factory closing.
Believe me at night I've prayed.
But those big old wheels keep on turning
in the factory where teachers are made.

So, now you know where teachers come from,
you couldn't really make it up.
They're not produced in ivy-clad universities.
It's in a factory down by the cut.

The Seagull Who Nicked My Chips

(Inspired by a poem by Nick Toczek)

The sun was shining high in the sky,
ice-creams and lollies were being sold nearby.
I had only placed it between my lips,
he dived so low; he nicked my chips.

Mum was giving us a right good earful.
"Beware kids, of those pesky seagulls."
I watched a gull doing his tricks.
Like a guided missile he nicked my chips.

He squawked, he screeched.
He swooped and dived.
Scared me to death, nearly ate me alive.
Who?
The seagull who nicked.
The seagull who nicked.
The seagull who nicked my chips.

Chips, fudge and homemade pies.
Stolen there, right before our eyes.
Candy floss and toffee apples.
Buying food is one big gamble.

Gran went mad and screamed out loud,
"Those blessed seagulls are all around."
I watched a gull doing his tricks
as straight as an arrow he nicked my chips.

He squawked, he screeched.
He swooped and dived.
Scared me to death, nearly ate me alive.
Who?
The seagull who nicked.
The seagull who nicked.
The seagull who nicked my chips.

Families flee in utter chaos.
"Come on kids they're sure to get us.
Cover your chips. Cover your crisps.
Hide whatever goes in your lips!"

Mum was frantic and full of fear.
"Those flipping seagulls are getting near."
I watched a gull doing his tricks.
With stealth and guile, he nicked my chips.

He squawked, he screeched.
He swooped and dived.
Scared me to death, nearly ate me alive.
Who?
The seagull who nicked.
The seagull who nicked.
The seagull who nicked my chips.

Buckets and spades our only weapons
Every summer battle stations.
Dad screamed and dropped his coffee,
"Quick, quick, it's nicked my lolly."

Every summer, worried and anxious.
We're just used as target practice.
The only thing the seagulls promise,
is every day they'll poop upon us.

He squawked, he screeched
He swooped and dived.
Scared me to death, nearly ate me alive.
Who?
The seagull who nicked.
The seagull who nicked.
The seagull who nicked my chips.

The Society of Funny Names

Tiny Tamara Fozzletop
was fond of fun and games.
She had a thought, to start a club
for people with funny names.

Little Johnny Twinklebottom
was the first upon the list.
Next was Una Umble Uffington
and a girl called Olivia Twist.

The Bushington twins, Billy and Bobby
completed an online form.
They were joined soon after by Jessica Jax
and her little dog called 'Norm.'

Sanjeet McStringy was first to arrive
to organise the tables and seating.
At 7.30pm last Tuesday night
Bicknesh Blong began the meeting.

Captain Colin Chuggly-Chambers
a man with looks and brains.
Announced, "I declare this meeting open,
The Society of Funny Names."

Told You I Was Ill

My Dad says that
I'm a hypochondriac.
Does he really know
I'm having a heart attack?

I'm in my bed
and I've just awoken.
My back's so sore.
I wonder. Is it broken?

My tongue
has turned a funny colour.
I'm very worried
I won't make the summer.

I've searched the Internet
and entered my symptoms.
It says I have a rare
life-threatening condition.

I've planned my funeral
and written my will.
I've ordered my headstone.
Saying, 'Told you I was ill'

I've caught the German Measles
or is it Spanish flu.
My tummy's bubbling
I need a ... doctor.

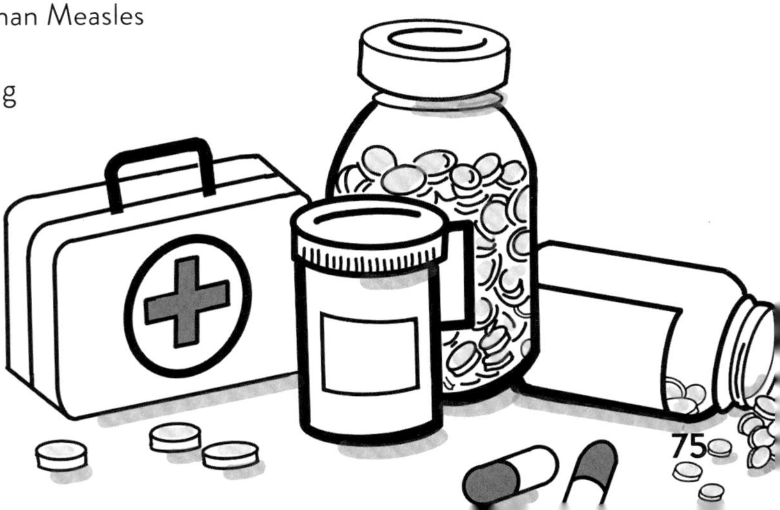

Two Hits to Who?

Two Tawny owls,
were both playing pool.
Ollie, the eldest,
was a stickler for rules.

He had beady wide eyes
and didn't miss a thing.
Awarding points
if the ball touched a wing.

If a foul was committed,
what a hullabaloo!
He'd shout, "Right, that's two hits!"
Yeah, two hits? But two hits to who?

Uncle Fish

When I was young I had one wish.
To swim as fast as my Uncle Fish.
He's the fastest thing I've ever seen.
To swim like him is my only dream.

He swims each night just after dinner.
They say he's faster than a river.
He out-swam a shark last year in Devon.
Then gave a dolphin a swimming lesson.

He's been world champion nine times or more.
Not bad considering he's eighty four.
He swims each day come rain or shine.
He's won Olympic gold about sixteen times.

Last week he received a knighthood.
He's now known as Sir Richard Wood.
But I don't buy into any of this.
He's just my hero - My Uncle Fish.

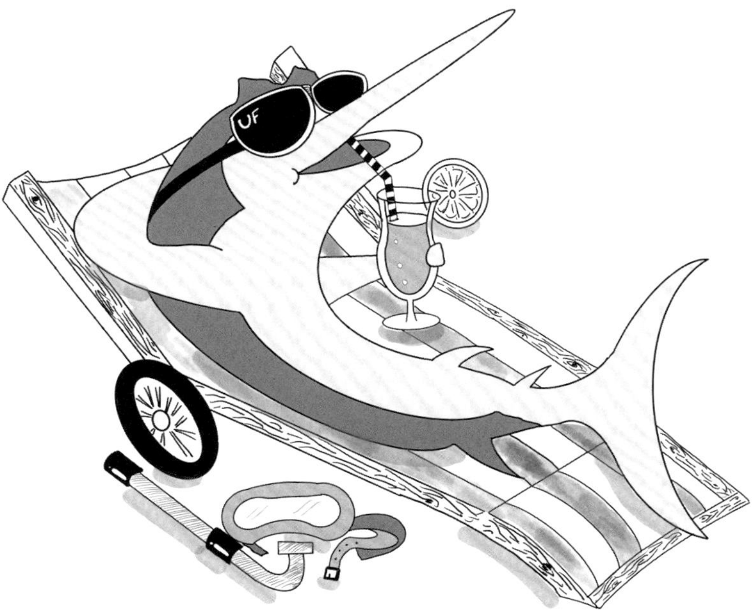

Vampires for Hire

'Vampires for hire,'
read a sign upon the door.
I wasn't sure when I stepped inside
Spying blood upon the floor.

'Count Me In' and 'Pain in the Neck.'
Were the signs upon the counter.
Then a tall, pale man with outstretched hand.
Said, "Hello I'm the company founder."

I'm not being rude but the way he moved.
He seemed to float no doubt.
He lifted his head and proudly said,
"I am Mr Tooten, but you can call me Count."

Count Tooten what an unusual name.
It sort if made me giggle.
Upon his hat was a big round badge,
with a vampire bat in the middle.

I'm no boffin but I spied a coffin.
In an alcove just at the side.
There inside was a fully dressed bride.
He smiled, "This is Doris, my wife!"

"What is it you actually sell in here?"
I managed to mumble a question.
"Gert lush, it's a proper job we do here boy!"
"It's alright," He smiled, "She's from Devon!"

"To save the confusion, it's blood transfusion."
Doris smiled, "I thinks that it's proper sweet.
We don't use syringes, test-tubes or pipes
Instead, we just use our teeth!"

They both smiled in unison.
Revealing fangs all shiny and bright.
I kid you not, I was out like a shot.
Leaving behind the Count and his wife.

Vicious Cycle

He shouts "Get back, get lost, don't come near!"
He fills his rider full of fear!
He's mean, horrid and really spiteful.
Don't ever try and ride the vicious cycle.

He really does such nasty things.
He'll spin his tyres and burn your shins.
He'll do a wheelie right over your toes.
and ring his bell when he hits your nose.

His handle bars will give you scars.
He'll try and push you in front of cars.
He has spikes sticking up from his saddle.
Oh, what an unpleasant way to travel.

He shouts "Get back, get lost, don't come near!"
He fills his rider full of fear!
He's mean, horrid and really spiteful.
Don't ever try and ride the vicious cycle.

Walking in the Woods

I was walking in the woods
But there was no one there.
I turned round quickly
And there was a bear!

So I ran and ran as fast as I could.
But I ran deeper and deeper, into the woods.

I was walking in the woods
and I heard someone crying.
I turned round quickly
and there was a lion!

So, I ran and ran as fast as I could.
But I ran deeper and deeper, into the woods.

I was walking in the woods
and I heard a twig break
I turned round quickly
and there was a snake!

So, I ran and ran as fast as I could.
But I ran deeper and deeper, into the woods.

I was walking in the woods
and the path got wider.
I turned round quickly
and there was a tiger!

So, I ran and ran as fast as I could.
But I ran deeper and deeper, Into the woods.

I ran and I ran before the beast pounced.
The very next thing, I was safe in my house.

What is Green?

What is green?
Green is the colour of beans and peas.
Some say it's the colour of jealousy.
Green is the colour of fresh cut grass.
In French it's vert, which is also grass.
Green is 'Go' on traffic lights.
Green is the colour of my true love's eyes.
Green is the colour of a dollar bill.
Green is my colour when I am ill.

What is Pink?

What is pink?
Pink is the colour of a cuddly pig
or a candy floss that's very big.

What is red?
Red is the colour of my dad's lips
or tomato sauce upon my chips.

What is orange?
Orange is the colour of a cheeky parrot.
or a really long and bendy carrot.

What is yellow?
Yellow is the colour of the sun
or a little chick behind its mum.

What is green?
Green is the colour of a lily pad
or a furious frog that's really mad.

What is blue?
Blue is the colour of the sky
or the colour of my truelove's eyes.

What is indigo?
Indigo is the colour of blueberry jam
that is lovingly made by my nan.

What is Violet?
Violet is the colour between purple and blue.
or a plump aubergine cut in two.

What is pink?
Pink is the colour of a cuddly pig
or a candy floss that's really big

What's the Difference?

We have fingers and they have tentacles.
They have laser eyes and don't need spectacles.
They use flying saucers instead of the bus.
That's the difference between aliens and us.

We drink milk and cans of pop.
They drink Blurst from the Planet Grock
They eat moon rocks and sonic dust
That's the difference between aliens and us.

We turn pink when we sit in the sun.
They're lime green with a bright blue bum.
They go invisible without any fuss.
That's the difference between aliens and us.

Who Would Be a Football Referee?

Who would ever want to be a football referee?
A question that has often bothered me.
I'm shouted at, kicked and sometimes punched.
All on a Sunday before my lunch.

I'm despised by the fans, called nasty names.
I'm accused every week of fixing games.
I've been hit in the face by a left footed volley.
Banged on the head with an old lady's brolly.

I've been tripped up by managers, as I ran down the line
and pelted with oranges by the fans at half time.
The insults I've had run well into the millions.
I've been chased by stray dogs and pooped on by pigeons.

Who would ever want to be a football referee?
A question that has often bothered me.
I'm shouted at, kicked and sometimes punched.
All on a Sunday before my lunch.

Why Do Dogs Sniff Each Other's Bums

I can speak French and count to ten.
Dix rhymes with geese but not with French Hen.
I can tell the difference between a mole and a ferret.
I can say metamorphosis but I can't really spell it.
But I can't understand really hard sums
or why dogs sniff each other's bums.

I know to do algebra, one has to be able.
But I was never good at my B times table.
I know I'll get stung if I wind up a wasp.
I know that in our house, mum is the boss.
But I can't understand how teeth stick in gums
or why dogs sniff each other's bums.

I can make toast with jam and butter.
I know a chisel is used by a sculptor.
I understand that penguins have knees
and that we all evolved from chimpanzees.
But I can't understand why worms look so glum
or why dogs sniff each other's bums.

Someone should tell them; it just isn't right.
Shaking hands is far more polite.
The Prime Minister in the House of Commons.
Should be warning dogs about sniffing bottoms.
When meeting royalty one must act refined.
We wouldn't talk about sniffing behinds!

So, take my advice before you get banned.
When meeting a friend offer your hand.
Have a hug or a cuddle whatever you fancy.
Do whatever you want that makes you feel happy.
Offer a handshake and make sure it's strong.
No more bum sniffing as it's seriously wrong.

Writer's Block

When I usually write a poem
my thoughts, they are a plenty.
It's with dismay, I sit today,
and admit that my mind is empty.

Everything's gone, a total void.
My ideas, they've all departed.
A barren land of emptiness.
I'm alone and broken-hearted.

My mind is empty, so is my heart.
I stare blankly at the clock.
My vibrant verses have all but vanished.
They call it 'Writer's Block!'

Not a single idea has said hello.
Nowt. Nothing. Nil.
Tumbleweed trundles past.
Zip. Zero, Zilch.

I wish my words would soon return.
I miss them so very much.
I'm now a redundant wordsmith.
I've lost the Midas touch.

Oh, hang on a moment, what was that?
I think, I've thunked a thought.
I'm not insane, I'm back in the game.
My gift is learned not taught.

Yvonne My Pet Stone

I have a pet stone,
her name is Yvonne.
I found her last Saturday
when mum drained the pond.

She was all green and slimy.
In desperate need of a scrub.
I'm talking about Yvonne.
Do you think I meant my mum?

Well, I took Yvonne inside
and gave her a nice warm bath.
Applied my favourite make up
and sprinkled her with talc.

Yvonne is my bestest pal
and never makes me sad.
She never ever gossips,
for which I'm truly glad.

She listens so intently
to my worries and woes.
Staying safe within my pocket
wherever I decide to go.